ULTIMATE TEDDY
B·E·A·R

THE LITTLE BOOK OF

CELEBRITY BEARS

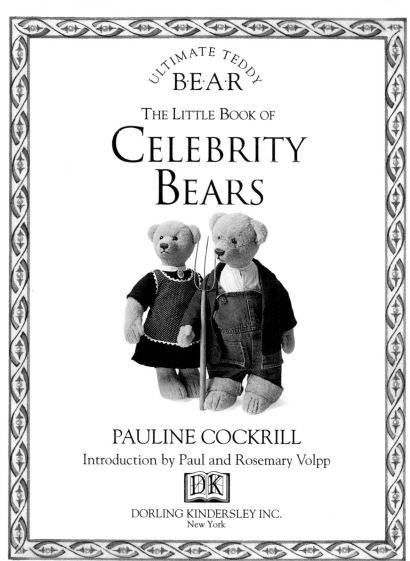

PAULINE COCKRILL

Introduction by Paul and Rosemary Volpp

DK

DORLING KINDERSLEY INC.
New York

A DORLING KINDERSLEY BOOK

PROJECT EDITOR Polly Boyd
ART EDITOR Vicki James
MANAGING EDITOR Mary-Clare Jerram
MANAGING ART EDITOR Gill Della Casa
PRODUCTION MANAGER Eunice Paterson
U.S. EDITOR Laaren Brown

FIRST AMERICAN EDITION, 1992
10 9 8 7 6 5 4 3 2 1

PUBLISHED IN THE UNITED STATES BY
DORLING KINDERSLEY, INC., 232 MADISON AVENUE
NEW YORK, NEW YORK 10016

COPYRIGHT © 1992 DORLING KINDERSLEY LIMITED, LONDON

ISBN 1-56458-082-2

Library of Congress Catalog Card Number 92-53229

Computer page make-up by The Cooling Brown Partnership, Great Britain
Text film output by The Right Type, Great Britain
Reproduced by Colourscan, Singapore
Printed in Hong Kong

❧ CONTENTS ❧

❧· INTRODUCTION ·❧
by Paul and Rosemary Volpp

This book is a celebration of the bears who have – over the years – given the most pleasure to the most people. You need not own one of these bears to feel a kinship to them and to recognize them as old friends. Their influence has crossed borders, oceans, and language barriers. Winnie the Pooh books by A.A. Milne have been translated into 20 languages, including Latin and Greek. And Pooh bear is loved in every language! He is joined by other "literary bears" such as Paddington, Rupert, and actor Peter Bull's Bully Bear.

In our collection on Buck Hill, we have three teddy bears who have reached celebrity status for three very different, varied reasons. Aloysius was famous, first, for being owned by arctophile and actor Peter Bull, who originally named him Delicatessen in recognition of his long life in an American grocery store. Then, after he appeared in the television series "Brideshead Revisited," he

FIREMEN'S MASCOT
This rare 1906 Steiff saw active duty during the Blitz.

4

became a celebrated TV star. His name was then changed officially to Aloysius.

•❄•❄•

In the early 1980s, our bear Bo became a favorite with *Teddy Bear and Friends* magazine readers around the world. People who knew they would never own an antique teddy bear "adopted" him as their own. Bo received cards, letters, and even Christmas gifts from his friends in the bear world. Then he was invited by Jackie and Mike Brooks to attend Australia's first Doll and Teddy Convention. While there, he appeared on Australia's "Today" show, "Wide World of Sports," and the popular "The Midday Show."

PERSONALITY BEAR
Created in 1983 to honor the child star Shirley Temple.

•❄•❄•

One of the world's best-known bears at this point in time is our teddy Happy Anniversary. She is famous for being the most expensive bear in the world. We bought her at an auction at Sotheby's in London for $86,350. She now spends her time making public appearances to raise money for children's hospitals. It is our wish that eventually this is what she will be remembered for.

COMMEMORATIVE BEAR
This bear was created by Hermann to celebrate German reunification. In his bag he carries a piece of the Berlin Wall.

❊ Bo ❊
The Ultimate Teddy Bear

Cinnamon-colored mohair plush.

Circular black boot-button eyes set close together.

Center seam characteristic of some early Steiffs.

Soft muzzle, as wood-wool stuffing has disintegrated into sawdust.

Antique white cotton collar with metal stud.

Four black claws on each paw and foot stitched across mohair plush.

Beige felt footpads in near-mint condition.

HEIGHT: 24IN (61CM).

In the teddy bear world, Bo (a 1905 Steiff) is generally regarded as the consummate teddy. Indeed, his endearing expression has driven many teddy manufacturers to strive to capture the Bo "look." He now resides in Southern California with Happy (*see page 11*) and has made many appearances on television with his owners, Paul and Rosemary Volpp.

❦ CORONATION BEAR ❦
1953 Commemorative Bear

Red, white, and
blue mohair
plush.

Transparent
glass eyes with
black pupils.

Head and body
filled with kapok.

Muzzle filled with
wood-wool
stuffing.

Cardboard swivel
joints at limbs
and head.

Distinctive
Merrythought
blanket-stitched
claws.

Felt pads on
base of feet.

HEIGHT: 15IN (38CM).

The coronation of Queen Elizabeth II in 1953 resulted in the production of a wealth of coronation memorabilia. Like many other manufacturers of luxury goods, the toy companies were quick to pick up on this trend. In the year of the coronation, the British firm Merrythought Ltd. created this patriotic red, white, and blue bear for the occasion.

❧ PIERRE ❧

Prize-winning French Teddy Bear

Original orange glass eyes with black pupils fused to opaque glass beneath.

Whistle added by previous owners to look like a jester's rattle.

Long muzzle with sealing wax nose.

Upturned mouth stitched with black thread.

Original beige felt ruffs around neck, cuffs, and ankles.

Unusual jester's outfit of red and yellow mohair plush tipped with black.

Very worn brown mohair plush on woven beige backing.

Large flat feet reinforced with cardboard.

Five brown stitched claws.

HEIGHT:14IN (36CM).

This bear won "Best of Show" at the first International League of Teddy Bear Clubs held in Los Angeles, in 1985. The origins of this teddy bear, with its very unusual shape and coloring, are unknown, but his present owners suspect that Pierre was made in France in the early 1900s. Clown teddy bears became extremely popular c.1907–1920.

❧ GATTI ❧
Survivor of the Titanic

Ears, set wide apart, show signs of wear.

Original metal eyes painted black.

Mouth embroidered with black stitching.

Nose hand-embroidered with horizontal stitches.

Mohair plush in good condition.

Short-pile golden mohair plush.

Fully jointed head and limbs with internal metal frame.

Short and extremely straight arms and legs.

HEIGHT: 6IN (15CM).

One of the victims of the Titanic disaster of 1912 was Gaspare Gatti, the liner's catering manager. Among his few possessions recovered from the ship was this tiny bear which, amazingly, came out of the disaster unscathed. A born survivor, he later narrowly escaped damage during the bombing raids over London in World War II.

❧·VIRGINIA·❧
Forerunner of the Glass Eye Trend

Long, distinctly triangular face.

Blue glass eyes with black pupils.

Body filled with wood-wool stuffing.

Nose embroidered with horizontal stitching.

Limbs slightly shorter than those of German bears.

Honey-colored mohair plush.

Three claws stitched with black thread on each foot and paw.

Beige felt pads on feet and paws.

HEIGHT: 16IN (41CM).

his pretty little bear has no trademark (few of the early American teddy bears do), but her present owners, expert arctophiles, are convinced that she was manufactured by The Ideal Novelty & Toy Co., c.1914. As such, she is one of the first American bears to have glass eyes. Prior to 1914, the company used boot buttons, as did most manufacturers.

❧·HAPPY·❧
The World's Most Expensive Bear

Ears set wide apart in Steiff tradition.

Steiff button with raised lettering in left ear.

Large brown glass eyes with black pupils.

Nose hand-embroidered with brown thread.

Dual-colored mohair plush made specially for teddy bear industry.

Long, blunt, protruding muzzle.

Four brown claws stitched across mohair plush on each paw.

Large beige felt pads.

HEIGHT: 24IN (61CM).

In 1989, bear collector Paul Volpp gave Happy, a 1926 Steiff, to his wife, Rosemary, as a present for their wedding anniversary. He paid an astounding US $86,350 for Happy at Sotheby's in London – a record that still stands. Her origins, rarity, size, and condition, but most of all her endearing expression, account for the very high price paid.

❧ AMERICAN GOTHIC ❧
Farmer Bears Adapted from a Painting

Imitation boot-button eyes.

Brown vertically stitched nose.

Brown cotton polka-dot apron.

Beige mohair plush cut out from a unique pattern.

Farmer's traditional pitchfork.

Thumb indicated on beige felt paw.

Four stitched claws on each paw and foot.

HEIGHT: 19IN (48CM).

HEIGHT: 20IN (51CM).

At a teddy bear convention in 1990 in Clarion, Iowa, teddy bear artists were asked for their interpretation of Grant Wood's famous painting *American Gothic*, which depicts rural, Mid-western life in the 1930s. The winner was Barbara Conley from San Jose, California, who won first prize for this charming teddy bear couple.

❧ SIR MORTIMER ❧
Celebration of a Roman Town

Large, rounded ears set wide apart on head.

Safe, plastic, lock-in eyes.

Black vertically stitched nose at tip of long, pointed muzzle.

Bow tie gives him the look of a British academic.

A speckled mixture of brown, black, and beige synthetic plush.

Pads made with an orange velvet-like fabric.

HEIGHT: 18IN (46CM).

Susan Rixon, of Nonsuch Soft Toys, produced this limited-edition teddy bear in 1990 to celebrate the centenary of the excavation of Silchester, a Roman town close to her home in Berkshire, England. Sir Mortimer is named after both the eminent British archaeologist, Sir Mortimer Wheeler, and the nearby village of Mortimer, in Berkshire.

❧ RUPERT BEAR ❧
World-Famous Cartoon Bear

White synthetic fur fabric with synthetic stuffing.

Safe plastic lock-in eyes.

Black vertical stitching on nose.

Embroidered black inverted Y-shaped mouth.

Traditional red knitted sweater.

Red winter coat unique to this 1986 Special Edition bear.

Yellow and black checked scarf and trousers usually worn by Rupert.

Soft imitation-leather shoes tied with real laces.

HEIGHT: 16IN (41CM).

Rupert Bear was originally a cartoon character, created by Mary Tourtel in 1920 for the London Daily Express. He soon became a national institution in Britain and later captured the hearts of many other nations around the world. It was not long before Rupert Bear memorabilia was produced, and from the 1960s, he was widely available as a stuffed toy.

❧ CHRISTIAN GABRIEL ❧
Rare Early Steiff Bear

Elephant "button in ear" (early trademark of a raised elephant).

Distinctive seam across top of head.

Shiny black boot-button eyes.

Large sealing wax nose.

Wood-wool-stuffed torso, head, and limbs.

Long limbs typical of early Steiff bears.

Beige mohair plush worn in places.

Five black claws stitched across each beige felt paw and footpad.

HEIGHT: 15IN (38CM).

Made by Steiff in 1903, this bear is very rare. Christian was made when Steiff was experimenting with teddy bear design, in particular the jointing system of their bears. Whereas earlier bears were made with a thread jointing system, Christian Gabriel has a rod that links his head and limbs. He also has a well-preserved sealing wax nose.

❧ KING ARTHUR ❧
Former Record Breaker at Sotheby's

Steiff button with raised lettering in left ear.

Large black boot-button eyes.

Nose indicated with beige stitches – a color always used on white Steiff bears.

Torso, head, and limbs stuffed with wood wool.

Long arms extend beyond legs.

Large beige felt pads on paws and feet.

HEIGHT: 30IN (76CM).

King Arthur, a c.1905 Steiff bear, is prized because of his excellent condition and stature – few early Steiff bears of such a large size survive. He broke all previous auction records for teddy bears when he was sold at Sotheby's, London, in October 1985 for US $5,872. Arthur is actually a white Steiff, but his fur has discolored over the years.

❧ · FRITZ · ❧

German Prisoner of War's Bear

Original brown boot-button eyes.

Black vertical stitching indicates nose.

Cap badge from the Royal Army Ordnance Corps.

Fully jointed body, head, and limbs.

Worn and discolored golden mohair plush.

Gray and pink hand-knitted jacket added by P.O.W.

Embroidered insignia taken from soldier's uniform.

1939 bronze German medal (War Merit Cross, Second Class).

Woven foot-pads.

HEIGHT: 11IN (28CM).

A t the end of World War II, this dusty bear was found under the floor of a Quonset hut that a German prisoner of war had occupied. On cleaning, Fritz was revealed to be a 1906 golden mohair-plush Steiff. Though his fur was discolored and worn, he was found in a dignified state, decorated with impressive German and British badges.

❦·ALFONZO·❦
Russian Princess's 1908 Steiff

Ears set wide apart, in tradition of early bears.

Steiff "button in ear" with raised lettering.

Horizontal stitching on nose slightly worn.

Small black boot-button eyes positioned close together.

Original orange Russian-style tunic.

Short rust-red mohair plush.

Four claws, each indicated with a single stitch.

Beige felt pads worn to reveal wood-wool stuffing.

HEIGHT: 13IN (33CM).

In 1908, the Grand Duke of Russia commissioned Steiff to make this unusual red bear for his daughter Princess Xenia Georgievna. In 1914, the Princess took her bear to England, where she stayed with relatives at Buckingham Palace. She never returned to Russia. Alfonzo, the gift from the father she was never to see again, became very dear to the princess.

❧ REBECCA ❧
Famed as a Porcelain Plate Decoration

Covered in soft honey-colored mohair plush.

Large brown glass eyes with black pupils and white ring around edge.

Shaved muzzle with black vertically stitched nose.

Body stuffed with wood wool – makes a crackling sound when squeezed.

Paws curve downward – a feature of Schuco bears.

Short stumpy arms and legs.

Beige felt pads on paws and feet.

HEIGHT: 21IN (53CM).

A 1930s Schuco Yes/No bear, Rebecca won her fame by appearing on a series of porcelain plates sold across the United States. All Yes/No bears have a head that nods or rotates when the bear's tail is moved up and down or from side to side. Schuco stands for Schreyer & Co., a German toy manufacturer that was established in 1912.

❊·RICHARD·❊
Richard Steiff's Replica of an Early Prototype

White label indicates the model is a replica.

Ears set wide apart.

Design of this bear unchanged from 1905–1951.

Replica black boot-button eyes.

Long jointed arms – a distinguishing feature of early Steiff bears.

Short-pile gray mohair plush used on only a few early prototypes.

Felt footpads with signature and date.

HEIGHT: 13IN (33CM).

This 1983 bear is a replica of a prototype developed by Richard Steiff in 1905. (The original bear was placed in the Steiff factory archives in Germany in the 1940s.) The bear's beige felt footpads carry the signature of Hans Otto Steiff, great-grand-nephew of Margarete Steiff, the original inspiration behind this highly successful family company.

❖·ALOYSIUS·❖
Sebastian's Bear in "Brideshead Revisited"

Triangular face, a distinctive feature of early Ideal bears, has lost its shape.

Large black boot-button eyes.

New black stitching on nose.

Scarf given by the wife of Anthony Andrews, a star in "Brideshead Revisited."

Red stitching on tongue added at a later date.

Only surviving original paw pad; others were replaced by Peter Bull.

Worn beige mohair plush patched with suede.

HEIGHT: 24IN (61CM).

For many years, Aloysius (a 1904–1905 Ideal) sat on a shelf in a New England grocery store. When his elderly owner saw Peter Bull (*see page 35*) talking about teddies on television, she decided he should inherit Aloysius. This bear won fame when he was featured in the television adaptation of Evelyn Waugh's classic *Brideshead Revisited*.

❧·POLITICAL BEAR·❧
Teddy Roosevelt Campaign Button

Eyes suggested with tiny black beads.

Bear worn by Roosevelt's supporters on lapels.

Small black sealing wax nose.

Low-grade white mohair plush; brown and beige plush also available.

Campaign ribbon, worn by diligent party workers.

Delicate paper paws are rare, as few have survived.

HEIGHT: 3IN (8CM).

In 1902, President Teddy Roosevelt went out hunting in Mississippi. His only chance of a kill was a bear cub that his trackers tied to a tree; he refused to shoot it. Thus he became associated with bears. In 1903, "Teddy's Bear," the first American soft-toy bear, was made. This bear *(above)* was a mascot in the 1904 presidential election campaign.

❧ ANNIVERSARY BEAR ❧

Sixty Years in the Business

Large rounded ears set on sides of head.

Pale golden mohair plush with feather finish.

Pointed clipped muzzle.

Trademark on Union Jack label stitched to right foot-pad.

Safe plastic lock-in eyes positioned next to muzzle.

Limited edition tag set in side seam.

Large beige Draylon pads.

HEIGHT: 18IN (46CM).

ounded in 1930, Merrythought Ltd. is one of the oldest surviving stuffed-toy manufacturers in Britain. In 1990, the company produced this limited-edition teddy bear to celebrate its 60th anniversary. With his pointed, clipped muzzle, large ears, humped back, and long limbs, he resembles the models produced by Merrythought in the 1930s.

❧ PADDINGTON BEAR ❧
Well-Loved Storybook Bear

Safety pin in sou'wester (prohibited in 1989 for safety reasons).

Safe plastic nose. (U.S. Paddington has an embroidered nose.)

Safe amber and black plastic eyes.

Golden mod-acrylic plush.

Polyester and acrylic fiber stuffing.

Unjointed body.

Plastic Wellington boots added by designer Shirley Clarkson. These were later written into the stories.

On tag: DARKEST PERU Via PADDINGTON To London, England 5m

HEIGHT: 20IN (51CM).

Paddington first appeared in 1958 as an illustration in the children's book *A Bear Called Paddington*, by Michael Bond. More Paddington Bear stories followed, as well as a television series, and this lovable bear shot to fame worldwide. Shirley Clarkson, of the British company Gabrielle Designs, created this interpretation of Paddington in 1972.

❧ AUNT LUCY ❧
Paddington Bear's Aunt on a Visit from Peru

Plastic spectacles on a chain.

Safe plastic nose.

Traditional Peruvian black bowler hat.

Woolen shawl around shoulders.

Polyester and acrylic fiber stuffing.

Tag pinned to shawl stating Lucy's address.

Long-pile gray mod-acrylic plush.

Traditional peasant-style gingham skirt.

White cotton bloomers cover legs.

HEIGHT: 20IN (51CM).

This eccentric-looking bear is Aunt Lucy, who, in Michael Bond's Paddington Bear stories, looked after Paddington in darkest Peru before his departure for England. Aunt Lucy is produced from the same materials as Paddington, but her fur is darker and she is wearing a traditional Peruvian costume. She was designed by Shirley Clarkson in 1976.

❧ PRINCE OF LOVE ❧
Romantic Novelist's Bear

Eyes originally glass, now replaced with wool.

Mouth can be opened by operating lever at back of head.

Pink satin bow tied around neck.

Fully jointed body.

Paw pads, originally rexine, were repaired with velvet.

Soft stuffing, probably kapok or sub (cotton waste).

Short-pile golden mohair plush worn away in places.

Bright, colorful costume jewelry decorates Miss Cartland's bear.

HEIGHT: 16IN (41CM).

This bejeweled bear once belonged to the English novelist Barbara Cartland. In 1988, he was loaned to the Teddy Bear Museum at Stratford-upon-Avon, England, where he is displayed with Barbara Cartland's poem: "I am a special teddy bear / I am very particular what I wear / My diamonds gleam like the stars above / As really I am the Prince of Love."

❧ · HORATIO · ❧
The Haunted Bear

Rounded ears set wide apart on either side of head.

Black boot-button eyes.

Brown inverted V-shaped mouth.

Rectangular nose with brown vertical stitching.

Long narrow arms typical of German bears of the period.

Golden mohair plush worn in places.

Large oval feet typical of early German bears.

Felt footpads with replacement stitching.

HEIGHT: 20IN (51CM).

ysterious tales of supernatural happenings surround this bear. Made in Germany c.1910, he was owned by sea captain Thomas Milligan. Since Milligan's death in 1951, strange sightings have been reported: his ghost has frequently been seen with Horatio, and it's said the aroma of the captain's tobacco fills the air when Horatio is near.

❦ WINNIE THE POOH ❧
Well-Loved Fictional Bear

Amber and black glass eyes.

Head filled with kapok stuffing, hence he is referred to as "bear of little brain."

Mohair plush on muzzle clipped.

Nose embroidered with brown stitching.

Inverted V-shaped mouth embroidered with brown stitching.

Replacement patches and stitching on paw and footpads.

Fully jointed body filled with kapok.

Long-pile golden mohair plush.

HEIGHT: 18IN (46CM).

One of the most famous of fictional bears, Winnie the Pooh was based on a real teddy bear belonging to author A. A. Milne's son, Christopher Robin. Pooh was sent to his American publisher, E. P. Dutton, when Milne died. Since 1987, Pooh has been on public display at the Donnell Library Center of The New York Public Library.

❧ PAW TUCKET ❧
Award-Winning Collector's Bear

Dual-colored dark brown and gray synthetic plush.

Shaved synthetic plush on muzzle.

Hard oval nose in black leather.

Beige suede tongue matches insides of ears.

Black leather pads on paws and feet.

Director's signature indicates limited edition.

HEIGHT: 17IN (43CM).

Gund, founded in Connecticut in 1898, was among the first of the stuffed-toy manufacturers to capitalize on the growing demand for teddies. Still in business, and now based in New Jersey, Gund creates some bears especially for the collector's market. In 1991 the company won the Toby Award, organized by *Teddy Bear and Friends* magazine, for this bear.

·&· AMELIA BEARHEART ·&·
The Bear that Inspired a Collection

Plastic flying goggles.

Black plastic eyes.

Body stuffed with shredded synthetic foam.

Brown imitation leather hat.

Aviator's scarf. (This bear is named after Amelia Earhart, who, in 1932, became the first woman to fly solo across the Atlantic.)

Unjointed arms and legs.

Cotton flying suit.

Pale blue nylon plush.

HEIGHT: 20IN (51CM).

This is the first teddy bought by Rosemary Volpp. With some time to spare, Mrs. Volpp wandered into a store where Amelia, a 1979 North American Bear Co. teddy, caught her eye. When it was suggested that she buy Amelia, the last of her kind in California, she said, "I don't collect bears." Today she and her husband, Paul, own over 5,000!

❧·MR. WHOPPIT·❧
The World's Speediest Bear

Pointed ears lined with blue felt.

Amber glass eyes with black pupils.

Motif added by Donald Campbell, who named all his vehicles "Bluebird."

Triangular nose embroidered with black stitching.

Original red felt jacket with white buttons.

Golden mohair plush worn away with age.

Body filled with kapok – a light buoyant fabric.

Legs and feet made of blue felt match inside of ears.

HEIGHT: 9IN (23CM).

From 1956–1957, the stuffed-toy maker Merrythought made many Mr. Whoppits, but none led the life of this bear! He was owned by Donald Campbell, who broke many world speed records on both land and water. In 1967, he was killed on Coniston Water, England. His body was never discovered, but Mr. Whoppit was found floating on the water's surface.

❧·FIRE GUARD BEAR·❧

London Fire Brigade Mascot

Long-pile golden mohair plush in mint condition.

Center seam on head – typical of every 7th bear on Steiff production line.

Original black boot-button eyes.

White cotton child's outfit decorated with embroidery on waistband, cuffs, and collar.

Blue woolen bib added by the London Fire Brigade.

Armband, added by the London Fire Brigade, says "bomb reconnaissance."

FIRE GUARD

Original beige felt foot-pads, singed by fire.

HEIGHT: 23IN (58CM)

This heroic bear served as a mascot for the London Fire Brigade during the Blitz in World War II. A rare 1906 golden mohair-plush Steiff, he is in excellent condition except for his singed feet, which were injured in his firefighting missions. He now resides with Fritz and Horatio (*see pages 17 and 27*) at the Cotswold Teddy Bear Museum (*see page 39*).

❧ SHIRLEY TEMPLE ❧
Teddy Artist's Personality Bear

Brown plastic eyes with black pupils.

Black thread mouth, stitched to indicate broad smile.

Body, head, and limbs filled with kapok.

Locks of curly hair, possibly a doll's wig.

Baked molded black nose.

Generous lace ruffle around neck.

Red cotton polka-dot dress.

Beige synthetic plush.

HEIGHT: 8IN (20CM).

Teddy bear artist Bev Miller designed this bear in 1983 to honor the child star Shirley Temple, whose career in films began at the tender age of three. Known for her personality bears, Bev Miller has also made appealing limited-edition teddy bears of Laurel and Hardy, the Marx Brothers (Groucho, Chico, and Harpo), and President Roosevelt.

❧ · HAMLEYS BEAR · ❧
1988 Steiff Made Exclusively for Hamleys Toy Store

"Button in ear" trademark with white cloth tag used for special-edition bears.

Safe replica black boot-button eyes.

Black stitching indicates nose and mouth.

Fully jointed body allows free movement of limbs and head.

Body contains squeaker mechanism.

Black claws stitched across mohair plush.

Light beige felt pads on paws and feet.

HEIGHT: 10IN (25CM).

 n 1988, Hamleys, the world's oldest and largest toy store, based in London, commissioned Steiff to make a limited-edition teddy bear exclusively for it. Only 2,000 of these bears were manufactured, each with Steiff's trademark as well as a chest tag with Hamleys' name, logo, and the limited-edition number printed on the card.

❧ BULLY BEAR ❧

Inspired by a Bear Belonging to Actor Peter Bull

Flat rounded
ears sit squarely
on head.

Mohair and
wool plush with
cotton backing.

Safe amber and
black plastic
eyes.

Extremely long,
foxlike muzzle.

Peter Bull's
signature on
label.

Long arms that
curve upward
at the paws.

Large
stumpy
feet with
synthetic
velvet, tear-
shaped
pads.

Woven
label,
bearing the
House of
Nisbet
logo.

HEIGHT: 18IN (46CM).

One of the House of Nisbet's earliest teddies, Bully
Bear was made in 1981, inspired by a bear belonging
to actor Peter Bull. Peter Bull was largely responsible
for the tremendous revival of interest in teddy bears worldwide,
which ensued after the publication of his entertaining
and informative *Teddy Bear Book* in 1969.

❧ ROOSEVELT BEAR ❧
Caricature of an American President

Small black boot-button eyes set close together.

Horizonally stitched rectangular black nose.

Mouth opens and closes to show two small white teeth.

Red silk bow tied around neck.

Beige felt pads worn in places to reveal wood-wool stuffing.

Three black claws on each paw and foot stitched across golden mohair plush.

HEIGHT: 18IN (46CM).

In 1908, the Columbia Teddy Bear Manufacturing Co. made this bear, the Laughing Roosevelt, rather unkindly depicting the prominent teeth of Theodore Roosevelt. By pushing in the bear's stomach, the owner could open his mouth and make him laugh. Few remain in mint condition, as they have been played with, and damaged, over the years.

❧ HARMLES ❧
Kimbal Union Academy Mascot

Large black
boot-button eyes.

Worn mohair plush
on muzzle.

Worn stitching
on nose reveals
black felt
underlay.

All paw and
footpads
replaced
with new
beige felt.

Initials of
Kimbal Union
Academy
embroidered
across chest.

Four claws
stitched across
mohair plush.

Long limbs in
Steiff tradition.

HEIGHT: 24IN (61CM).

A large c.1905 Steiff teddy bear, Harmles was the mascot at the Kimbal Union Academy, a boy's preparatory school in New Hampshire, near Dartmouth College, before World War I. He lost his "button in ear" trademark; however, all Harmles's other features indicate that he is almost certainly a Steiff teddy bear.

·❧· BEAR OWNERS ·❧·

Dorling Kindersley would like to thank the following people, who generously lent their teddy bears for photography:

• Gyles Brandreth, Teddy Bear Museum, Stratford-upon-Avon, UK for Sir Mortimer 13, Prince of Love 26
• Gina Campbell for Mr. Whoppit 31
• Wendy and Colin Lewis, Cotswold Teddy Bear Museum, Broadway, Worcestershire, UK for Fire Guard Bear 4, 32; Berlin Wall Bear 5; Fritz 17; Horatio 27
• Donnell Library Center, New York Public Library, New York, USA, for Winnie the Pooh 28
• Pam Hebbs for Richard 20
• London Toy & Model Museum, London, UK for Paddington Bear 24, Aunt Lucy 25
• Merrythought Ltd. for Anniversary Bear 23
• Sheryl Nairn for Rupert Bear 14
• Ian Pout for Coronation Bear 7, Alfonzo 18
• Judy Sparrow, The Bear Museum, Petersfield, Hampshire, UK for Hamleys Bear 34, Bully Bear 35
• Paul and Rosemary Volpp for American Gothic Couple 1, 12; Christian Gabriel 2, 15; Pierre 3, 8; Shirley Temple 5, 33; Bo 6; Virginia 10; Happy 11; King Arthur 16; Rebecca 19; Aloysius 21, 39; Political Bear 22, 38; Paw Tucket 29; Amelia Bearhart 30, 41; Roosevelt Bear 36; Harmles 37
• Ankie Wild, Ribchester Museum of Childhood, Ribchester, Lancashire, UK for Gatti 9

Thanks also to Barbara Cartland, whose bear, Prince of Love, is on loan to the Teddy Bear Museum, Stratford-upon-Avon, UK.

❧ USEFUL ADDRESSES ❧

MUSEUMS

Franny's Teddy Bear Museum
2511 Pine Ridge Road
Naples, Florida 33942
☎ (813) 598-2711

Margaret Woodbury Strong Museum
1 Manhattan Square
Rochester, New York 14607
☎ (716) 263-2700

The Steiff Museum
Margarete Steiff GmbH
PO Box 1560
Alliin Straase 2
D-7928 Giengen (Brenz)
Germany
☎ (49) 7322-1311

MAGAZINES

The Teddy Bear and Friends
Hobby House Press
900 Frederick Street
Cumberland,
Maryland 21502
☎ (301) 759-3770

Teddy Bear Review
Collector Communications Corp.
PO Box 1239
Hanover, Pennsylvania 17331
☎ (717) 633-7333

❧ INDEX ❧

❧· ACKNOWLEDGMENTS ·❧

Dorling Kindersley would like to thank the following photographers for their contributions to this book: Jim Coit 1, 2, 3, 5 (top), 6, 8, 10, 11, 12, 15, 16, 19, 21, 22, 29, 30, 33, 36, 37, 38, 39, 41; Peter Anderson 4, 5, 17, 27, 32; Roland Kemp 7, 13, 14, 18, 20, 23, 24, 25, 26, 34; Lynton Gardiner 28; Matthew Ward 9, 31, 35.

We would also like to thank the following for their help: Jeanette Mall, Susan Thompson, and Helen Townsend for editorial help; Pauline Bayne, Ann Terrell, and Sam Grimmer for design assistance; Alastair Wardle and Peter Howlett for their DTP expertise; and Michael Allaby for the index. Our special thanks go to Paul and Rosemary Volpp for their patience and generous contributions to the book.

The author would like to thank Jane Domican and the sales staff of the soft toy department at Hamleys, London; Oliver Holmes and John Parkes at Merrythought Ltd.; Susan Rixon at Nonsuch Soft Toys; Shirley Clarkson of Gabrielle Designs; Jack Wilson; and Sylvia Cootes and staff at the Teddy Bear Museum, Stratford-upon-Avon, UK.

Border illustrations by Pauline Bayne.
Illustrated letters by Gillie Newman.